What Do Puppies Need?

A kid's guide to taking care of a new puppy!

 Written By Cheryl Allison Barber

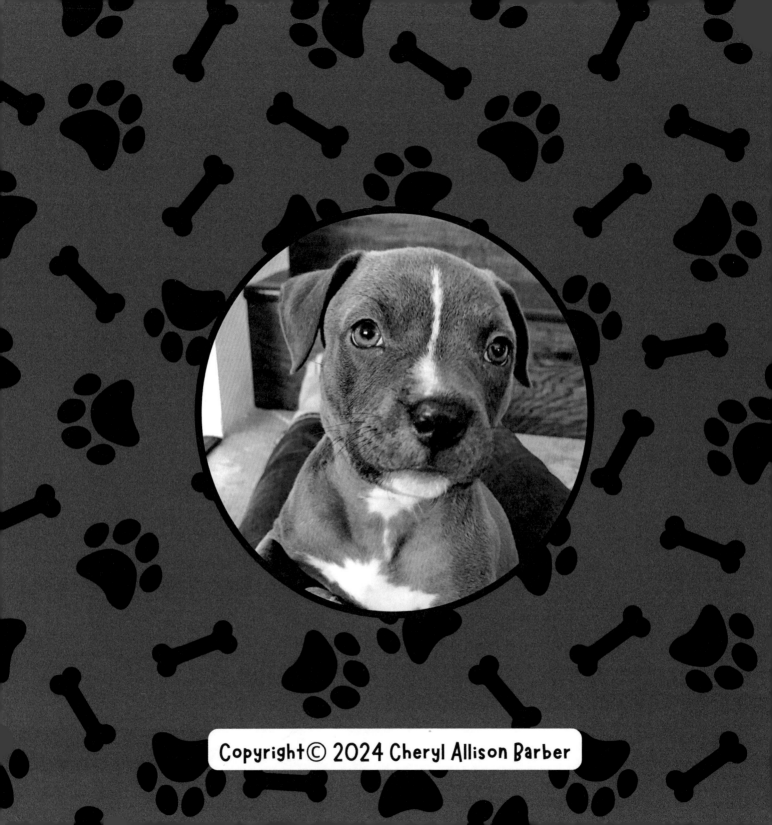

Puppies come in all shapes, sizes, and colors.

Even though they may look different, they are all SO cute!

When someone decides they want to adopt a puppy, they know it will be a big responsibility.

But what do puppies need?

Puppies need time to get used to their new home with you.

Puppies need lots of rest.

Puppies need to learn how to walk on a leash.

Puppies need special puppy food to help them grow big and strong.

Puppies need a bed.

Puppies need plenty of space to run.

Puppies need to go to the vet so they can stay healthy.

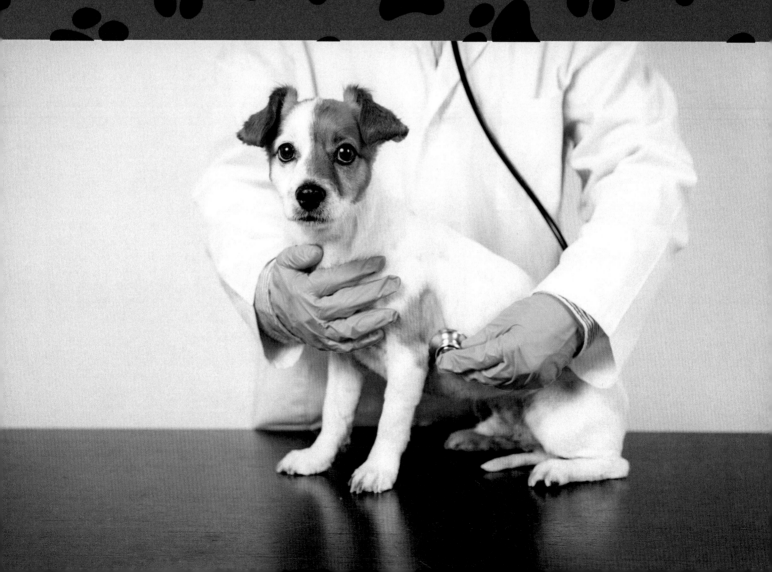

Sometimes puppies cry or whine.

Puppies need cuddles.

Puppies need belly rubs.

Puppies need fresh water.

Puppies need a cozy place to rest.

Sometimes puppies get dirty.

So puppies need to take baths.

Puppies have sharp teeth, and they might even chew something they shouldn't!

Puppies need something they can chew on that's just for them.

Puppies need toys to play with.

Puppies need plenty of exercise.

Some puppies like to play fetch!

Puppies do silly things because they are babies!

Puppies need patience to learn.

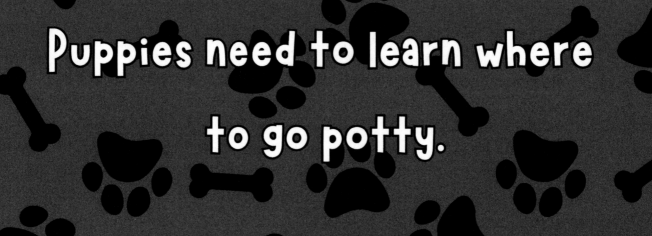

Puppies need to learn where to go potty.

Some puppies can learn commands and tricks.

Puppies need a collar and a tag with a phone number, just in case they get lost.

But most of all...
Puppies need LOVE!

A Note From The Author

My sweet readers...
While puppies are simply adorable and irresistible, always remember they are a life long commitment. When you decide to adopt a puppy, they should be able to spend their entire life with you! They will cherish your love and love you back unconditionally. That is the best part!

xoxo

Made in United States
North Haven, CT
26 February 2024

49227006R00020